Playground Games

Contents **Page**

Hide and Seek	2-3
Hopscotch	4-5
Hoops	6-7
Follow the Leader	8-9
Skipping	10-11
Marbles	12-13
Leap Frog	14-15
Ball games	16

written by Pam Holden

Do you like to play hide and seek in the playground?

hide and seek

Are you good at hiding?

Do you like to play a game of hopscotch at school?

Are you good at
hopping and counting?

Do you like playing with hoops in the playground?

Can you make a hoop go round and round?

hoops

Do you like to play follow the leader at school?

You can be the leader for this game.

follow the leader

Do you like to play games with ropes?

Are you good at
skipping and jumping?

skipping

Do you like to play a game of marbles at school?

Have you got some marbles to play with?

marbles

Do you like playing leapfrog?

You can jump over each other in this game.

leapfrog

Do you like to play games
with balls in the playground?
Yes, we do!